Effective Strategies for Maximizing Workforce Efficiency

Demariane T. Moreau

All rights reserved. Copyright © 2023 Demariane T. Moreau

Funny helpful tips:

Life is a dance of change; move with grace, adaptability, and joy.

Maintain a culture of recognition; appreciating efforts boosts morale.

Effective Strategies for Maximizing Workforce Efficiency : Proven Techniques to Boost Workforce Performance and Drive Unmatched Productivity

Life advices:

Stay vigilant about your digital footprint; online privacy is crucial in today's world.

Stay authentic; your unique essence is your strength.

Introduction

Navigating the intricacies of workforce management requires a comprehensive understanding of its various dimensions. This guide offers a roadmap, delving into the core aspects of forecasting, scheduling, monitoring, and optimizing productivity metrics.

Forecasting, the cornerstone of effective workforce management, is your starting point. Uncover the essence of forecasting – the art of predicting future workforce needs. Recognize its significance as a strategic tool in aligning your workforce with your organization's goals. Understand the different types of forecasting, from trend analysis to seasonality assessment, each playing a crucial role in shaping your management strategies.

Dive into the realm of forecasting techniques, honing your ability to make accurate predictions. Master the art of scheduling and rostering, ensuring that your workforce is optimally allocated. Explore Erlang, a potent tool for determining staffing requirements in dynamic environments. Gather tips, tricks, and essential facts that empower you to excel in scheduling, keeping your workforce synchronized and efficient.

In the realm of real-time management, real-time adherence is your guiding star. Unravel its significance in maintaining operational efficiency and addressing unforeseen disruptions promptly. Embrace the petals of real-time management – monitoring, seat capacity management, and seat planning. These components form the bedrock of real-time operational excellence, ensuring that your workforce's actions align seamlessly with your objectives.

Productivity metrics and formulas are your instruments of measurement and analysis. Understand their importance as yardsticks for assessing workforce performance. Delve into the world of productivity metrics, gaining insights into how they can be harnessed to boost efficiency. Uncover a treasure trove of proven techniques and strategies in workforce management, arming yourself with the tools to overcome challenges and optimize your workforce's potential.

As you navigate this guide, you'll uncover the intricacies of workforce management, equipping yourself with a comprehensive toolkit. From mastering forecasting to crafting efficient schedules, from real-time management to analyzing productivity metrics, each section adds to your mastery. So, embark on this journey with the assurance that you're on the path to creating a harmonious and high-performing workforce, an essential ingredient for any organization's success.

Contents

Chapter 1: Forecasting 1
    What is Forecasting? 2
    What is the Importance of Forecasting? 2
    Types of Forecasting 3
    Trend Analysis 13
    Seasonality analysis 15
    Forecasting Techniques 16

Chapter 2: Scheduling and Rostering 23
    Erlang 30
    Tips, Tricks & Facts about Scheduling 39

Chapter 3: Real Time Adherence 41
    Petals of Real Time Management 42
    Monitoring 42

Chapter 4: Seat Capacity Management 45
    Seat Planning 46

Chapter 5: Productivity Metrics & Formulas 57
    Importance of metrics 58

Chapter 6: More Tips and Tricks on proventechniques and Strategies in Workforce management 65

Conclusion 71

Chapter 1: Forecasting

What is Forecasting?

Forecasting is the process of predicting or estimating a future event or trend. It uses the historical data to determine the direction of future trends. If you contemplate deeply, every business revolves around the process of forecasting. Retail industries work on the past data of customer likes or purchase trends; mining industries plan their output depending on the forecasted need for the future. In large-scale fishing, success depends on an accurate prediction of fish beds at any time of the year. Climate changes are adequately prepared for with the help of proper weather forecast. Likewise, the process of forecasting is involved when companies need to determine their budget allocation for an upcoming period. This is primarily based on the demand for the goods and services they offer, compared to the cost of producing them. In stock markets, investors utilize forecasting to determine the effects of contingencies on a company, such as sales expectations, variations in the price of shares of that company, etc. It also helps in the attainment of important benchmark for firms with a long-term perspective of operations.

Stock analysts use various forecasting methods to determine the future movement of a stock's price. They might look at revenue and compare it to economic indicators or may look at other indicators, such as the number of new stores a company opens or the number of orders for the goods it manufactures. Economists use forecasting to extrapolate how trends, such as GDP or unemployment, will change in the coming quarter or year. In BPOs and other ITES companies, historical business trends are used to predict their future states which, among other things, include the volume of workload, future costs, and estimated revenues and so on.

What is the Importance of Forecasting?

All businesses and organizations depend on an accurate or near-accurate grasp of future events. Not only that, no entity can survive without a sense of projection; including human beings. The human body comes as an available reference where the eyelids are shut at the anticipation of a foreign object. If you are aware of the challenges coming in a couple of days, adequate counter-actions are potent enough to allay the apprehensions. Likewise, the art of forecasting is valuable to the conciliation of future conflicts.

The art of forecasting helps the organization to identify and quantify the cyclic and seasonal variation components of business volumes (customers) with their periodicity (annual, monthly, weekly or daily). Without a thorough understanding of these factors, it is likely that the planning process will result in poor customer satisfaction as well as overstaff, which would in turn lead to an unnecessary increase in labor costs for the organization. You need to know how many customers are going to reach out to you in a specific duration so that you can be ready to service all of them with 100% Customer Satisfaction.

Types of Forecasting

Forecasting is classified into three types: Short Term forecast, Mid Term Forecast, and Long Term forecast. Short term forecasting is catered for the predictions of trends within short frames like on a weekly basis or within the interval of minutes. Mid-term forecast considers 12 to 13 weeks while long-term forecast gives 6 to 12 months ahead of the business volume.

Short Term forecasting

Short Term forecasting helps to predict the immediate future of a business volume. In addition, these forecasts will give data at interval level (hereafter, 30mins is one interval). In this category, accuracy is a key factor since there is not enough time for rebound in case of mistakes.

For every forecast, historical data is required. Let us assume that you were tracking all customers who make a call every 30mins. With a two-year data, it is possible to predict the number of customers who would call from the 6th week onwards.

Short Term Forecasting process (or Interval Level Forecasting) is performed every week; it uses the historical data and the weekly transaction volume data as inputs. In the preceding example, the number of customers who called your business can be referred to as Offered Calls/Customers whereas the customers whom you were able to provide service will be called Handled Customers. Therefore, the customers who were offered but not handled will be termed Abandoned Customers. Assuming that you would get approx. 200 calls next week (method to predict these weekly numbers would be analyzed elsewhere), there are two parameters with short term forecasting.

1. What day of the week are you going to get the numbers?
2. During what time of the day are you going to get a number of customers?

Firstly, let us find what volume of transaction on certain days of the week. For that, we need to look at the history of the data we have for last 4 weeks and sum up the target days to get the percentage contribution to the total volume. (If your business is stable, then get more data as it affects the accuracy). The calculation is detailed as follows:

Step 1: *Add up all the target days.'*

	C	D	E	F	G	H	I	J	K	L
1	Week Details	Sun	Mon	Tue	Wed	Thu	Fri	Sat	Total	
2	4th Last Week	2	43	34	14	34	3	3	133	
3	3rd Last Week	5	38	33	20	33	3	2	134	
4	2nd Last Week	4	35	32	15	35	53	1	175	
5	Last Week	9	45	36	18	37	7	5	157	
6	Sum	=SUM(D2:D5)		135	67	139	66	11	599	
7										

Step 2: *Once you have the total, find the Percentage of volume, which has come in each day of the week.*

	C	D	E	F	G	H	I	J	K	L
1	Week Details	Sun	Mon	Tue	Wed	Thu	Fri	Sat	Total	
2	4th Last Week	2	43	34	14	34	3	3	133	
3	3rd Last Week	5	38	33	20	33	3	2	134	
4	2nd Last Week	4	35	32	15	35	53	1	175	
5	Last Week	9	45	36	18	37	7	5	157	
6	Sum	20	161	135	67	139	66	11	599	
7	Day of the Week	=/$K$6		23%	11%	23%	11%	2%	100%	

Step 3: *Split the weekly volume to Day-level with this percentage we arrived at. Simply, the multiplication between the day of the week distribution and total week's volume will give you the daily volume forecast.*

	A	B	C	D	E	F	G	H	I	J
1	Week Details	Sun	Mon	Tue	Wed	Thu	Fri	Sat	Total	
2	Day of the Week Factor	3%	27%	23%	11%	23%	11%	2%	100%	
3	Next Week Volum	=B2*$I$3		45	22	46	22	4	200	
4										
5										

Hurray! You have successfully forecasted day level volume from a weekly record. Now let us see how to split the day level volume to

Interval level Data (30mins) which would in turn answer the second question above.

Once we have the day level distribution forecast, the percentage of the time of the day pattern is to be calculated next. The process is very simple and similar to the previous method except for a minor change i.e., The Percentage allocation for each half hour of the interval is determined after applying smoothening forecasting methods like Moving Weighted Average method/Exponential Smoothening method. (These are explained in the forecasting Techniques in later pages):

Step 1: *Need to fix a weighted value for each week. If we are taking 4 weeks, depending on the week's confidence, you can give weightage. Just ensure 100% is the overall weightage added together. Also, 10-20-30-40 is an ideal weightage taken.*

	A	B	C	D	E	F	G	H	I	J
1	Time (GMT)	Weightage	9:00	9:30	10:00	10:30	11:00	11:30	12:00	12:30
2	Mon (Jul 7)	10%	3	10	11	19	30	49	50	30
3	Mon (Jul 14)	20%	2	11	13	22	35	52	55	29
4	Mon (Jul 21)	30%	3	15	12	23	28	49	48	26
5	Mon (Jul 28)	40%	4	13	11	20	35	50	60	30

Step 2: *Multiply weekly values against the weightage given.*

NOW =($B$5*E5)+($B$4*E4)+($B$3*E3)+($B$2*E2)

	A	B	C	D	E	F	G	H
1	Time (GMT)	Weightage	9:00	9:30	10:00	10:30	11:00	11:30
2	Mon (Jul 7)	10%	3	10	11	19	30	49
3	Mon (Jul 14)	20%	2	11	13	22	35	52
4	Mon (Jul 21)	30%	3	15	12	23	28	49
5	Mon (Jul 28)	40%	4	13	11	20	35	50
6	MW Average		3	13	=($B$5*E5	21	32	50

Step 3: *Once the MW Average is calculated, we can use the same method to find the percentage of volume allocations. There you go!*

You have the interval level volume predicted.

Time (GMT)	Weightage	9:00	9:30	10:00	10:30	11:00	11:30	12:00	12:30	13:00	13:30	14:00	14:30	15:00	15:30	Total
Mon (Jul 7)	10%	3	10	11	19	30	49	50	30	30	27	20	15	10	5	309
Mon (Jul 14)	20%	2	11	13	22	35	52	55	29	28	25	18	12	8	3	313
Mon (Jul 21)	30%	3	15	12	23	28	49	48	26	28	24	15	10	7	5	293
Mon (Jul 28)	40%	4	13	11	20	35	50	60	30	29	24	19	14	8	4	321
MW Average		3	13	12	21	32	50	54	29	29	25	18	13	8	4	310
% Allocation	=C6/$Q$6	4%	7%	10%	16%	18%	9%	9%	8%	6%	4%	1%	1%	100%		

In the above example, the percentage of transaction arrival distribution at the interval level for Monday was obtained after applying moving weighted average for the last 4 week Mondays.

In cases where month-level forecasts are obtained at one month in advance, it would be converted to week-level and then to day-level using the method described above. Instances where day-end forecasts are obtained one month before time, there are chances of change in transaction arrival pattern in the most recent weeks. This will make the generated forecast less accurate. Hence, the forecast, which is generated using latest week's offered data tend to have higher forecast accuracy as it captures the recent changes in transaction arrival pattern in all areas of distribution. (If in January we got the forecast for the month of March, there is a high chance for the volume to vary during the month of February and consequently, a less accurate prediction is obtained. This won't be the case if that volume is predicted at the end of February for March.)

Cleaning of Data

Cleaning of historical data is an important step that needs to be performed to remove the effects of outliers caused due to outages and other abnormal failures. (All kind of outage impacts, software or hardware, are to be taken into account). This clearance process is to be set up to capture all types of outages from technology teams, vendors/clients, and Real time Adherence teams. Outliers can cause high forecast errors, especially when it occurs at the recent week of historical data, which is when data points are in the most recent period, which carries higher weightage. Any outlier data point's presence over a period of time will result in lesser weightage, and smoothening models like weighted moving average or exponential smoothening can recover the accuracy caused by outliers and return to correct trend. Forecast generated with outliers have implications for estimating seasonal factors hence outlier detection and removal is an important step required to improve the forecasting accuracy.

Cleaning of data at the day level:

Data points for the day and offered transactions for the same day of the week are plotted in scatter graph. The trend of the graph is analyzed by fitting a linear regression equation **(y=ax+b** where **a (Slope)** and **b (Intercept)** are constants with **R (as the correlation coefficient)** to the trend. If the data points diverge from overall pattern, the diverging data points are considered as outliers and are to be removed.

When performing the trend analysis outliers in data points limits, the fit of the linear regression equation and the coefficient of the determinant are always higher when outliers are not present. The square of the correlation coefficient R that is termed as the coefficient of determination R^2 measures the percentage of variation in the dependent variable (actual observed values) that is explained by the regression or trend line. It has a value between zero and one, with a high value indicating a good fit. The correlation coefficient, R, measures the strength and direction of linear relationships between two variables. It has a value between –1 and +1.

Below is the scatter graph showing the data points (transactions offered) for last nine Mondays. It can be seen from Graph - A is that there is an outlier existing on 15 June. When this is removed, the coefficient of determination R² increases from 0.2716 to 0.9969 as seen in Graph - B.

In simple terms, when we plot the data points in the graph, outliers can be observed in the graph, or from your experience, you will know the presence of a special cause data point, then you remove it proactively. That will do. Special causes are removed since the probability of occurrence of these events in future is less.

Graph A   **Graph B**

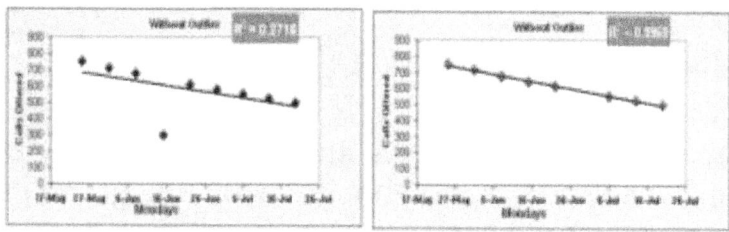

Cleaning of data at the Interval Level:

Interval level data cleanup is usually done by in-depth examination of the data. If an outlier is present for the major part of peak intervals, then that particular day entire data can be disregarded, and forecast should be generated with available/ accurate data points of other days. In such cases, we can also retain the intervals, which were not affected by outliers and include additional data points of previous weeks only for the intervals that have clear outliers. Certain nuances are present; therefore, discretion is advised.

When an outage occurs at certain intervals, there is always the possibility of immediate after-outage effect with higher transactions being offered at the following intervals. Hence, there is a need to consider these effects by proper documentation of inputs on outages as received from the vendor/client/monitoring teams.

A simple method of cleaning of data is by interval level comparison of the offered and forecasted data for the day affected by the outage. Below is the step-by-step explanation of how this is done at the interval level for a day affected by outages that will give more insights.

Step 1: *Compare the offered and forecasted data and identify intervals that are affected by the outage and the intervals that have the after-outage effect. These intervals show the data points having high divergence from the arrival pattern.*

Time (GMT)	9:00	9:30	10:00	10:30	11:00	11:30	12:00	12:30	13:00	13:30	14:00	14:30	15:00	15:30	Total
Offered	37	43				92	82	80	15	18	10	10	7	11	489
Forecasted	39	47	55	53	63	52	44	38	16	17	12	11	10	9	557

Step 2: *Calculation of Offered vs. Forecast for non-outage affected intervals. In the above example sum of offered transactions only for non-outage affected intervals is 235 transactions and sum of forecasted transactions only on non-outage affected intervals is 252 transactions. This gives an Offered vs. Forecast only for non-outage affected intervals as 235 / 252 = 93.25%*

Time (GMT)	6:00	6:30	7:00	7:30	8:00	8:30	9:00	9:30	10:00	10:30	11:00	11:30	12:00	12:30	13:00	13:30	14:00	14:30	15:00	15:30	Total
Offered	1	4	8	17	26	28	37	43				46	41	35	15	18	10	10	7	11	518
Forecasted	2	4	10	18	27	30	39	47	55	53	63	52	44	38	16	17	12	11	10	9	557

Step 3: *Cleaning of Outliers by applying the offered vs. forecast trend observed during non-outage hours on outage-affected hours.*

As in the above example:

At Interval 10:00 hours, forecasted transactions for that interval is multiplied with Offered vs. Forecast % observed during non-outage affected hours i.e. corrected data point for 10:00 hours is (55 Forecasted transactions) * (Off/For% of 93.25%) = 51 Transactions. Similar data cleaning process is done for other outage-affected intervals from 10:30 hours to 12:30 hours

Below is the graphical comparison how data will look like before and after removing the outliers. June 29 Monday had outage from 10:00 to 13:00 as shown in Graph-A, Graph-B shows data cleaned version of data points for June 29 during outage hours.

Graph A   Graph B

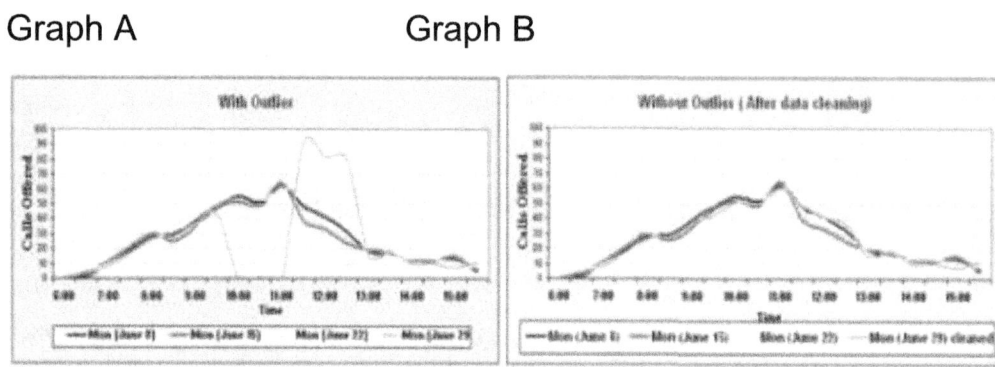

Other factors that affect forecast are Seasonality or Holidays. These impacts are to be recorded and used as inputs for tweaking. When a repetitive pattern is observed over some time horizon, the series is said to have seasonal behavior. Seasonal effects are usually associated with the calendar, and seasonal variation is frequently tied to yearly cycles (e.g. this pattern can be observed in the sales trend graph of a retails store, you will see a spike during Year-end sales or Christmas season).

The impact of certain holidays like Independence Day, Memorial Day and Christmas in previous years are studied for variations before the holiday, during holiday and after the holiday while they are calculated and applied to generate the forecast. It is generally noticed that transaction volumes are slightly higher before the holiday but very less during the holiday which shoots up immediately after the holiday.

Another important factor is the day of the week when the holiday occurs. If it occurs on the last year's Wednesday and this year's Friday, there will be no possible correlations. Impacts of holiday and after-holiday effects on weekdays and weekends are generally different. Alteration to the forecast needs to be applied based on the personal judgment during those respective days.

New product launches or other marketing strategies including process changes and modification, which are likely to affect forecasts, are also considered as inputs in the forecasting process.

Any new sales initiative that might influence the transaction volume/arrival patterns etc. are to be provided by the client to the forecasting team. These will be used as inputs for generating the forecasts. (These information are generally termed as Business Intelligence).

Mid Term Forecasting

Mid Term Forecasting shares the same principles with the foregoing category. It is performed weekly/bi-weekly/once every month and delivers as output a Midterm Forecast (for a minimum of 13 weeks up to maximum of 25 weeks look ahead). 13 weeks implies a 3 months head plan. The process will work on the historical inputs and business intelligence. If these inputs received are in the form of month-level, then it is converted into a week-level forecast, using the same methods we used in short term forecast. Ensure that cyclic and seasonal factors, which affect forecast and other business inputs, are to be recorded and incorporated while preparing the mid-term forecasts.

There are two main components that drive a Midterm forecast, Trend & Seasonality

Trend Analysis

Month: Trend is the rate of change in the transactions. While that trend can be upward or downward, in most businesses, trend simply means the growth rate. The ideal sample for calculating Growth Rate is Two Years Data.

Rate of Change is calculated as the difference between the Year's Month Volume and the previous year's dividend while it serves as the divisor.

Month	Year A	Year B	% Change
Jan	113000	132000	0.168
Feb	112000	128000	0.143
Mar	120000	140000	0.167
Apr	126000	146000	0.159
May	128000	152000	0.188

Jan Trend Rate = (132000 — 113000)/ 113000
= 0.168

Week: Monthly Forecast is required to be strewn to a weekly volume based on the pattern of the previous two years'. Below is the pictorial presentation of how the previous year's respective month weekly distribution percentage is split and factored into the forecasting process. The weeks that are considered for deriving the weekly forecast for April 2009 are:

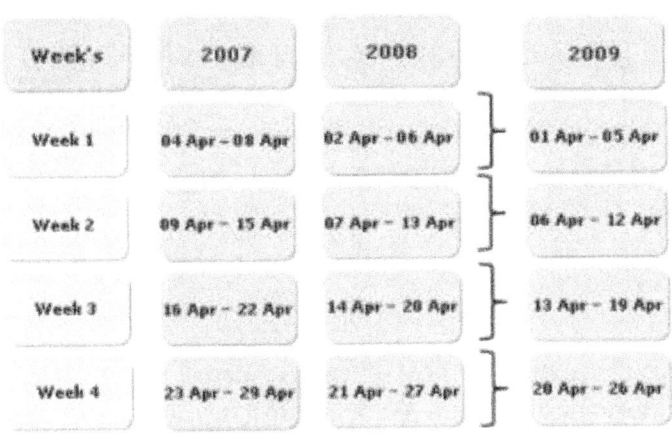

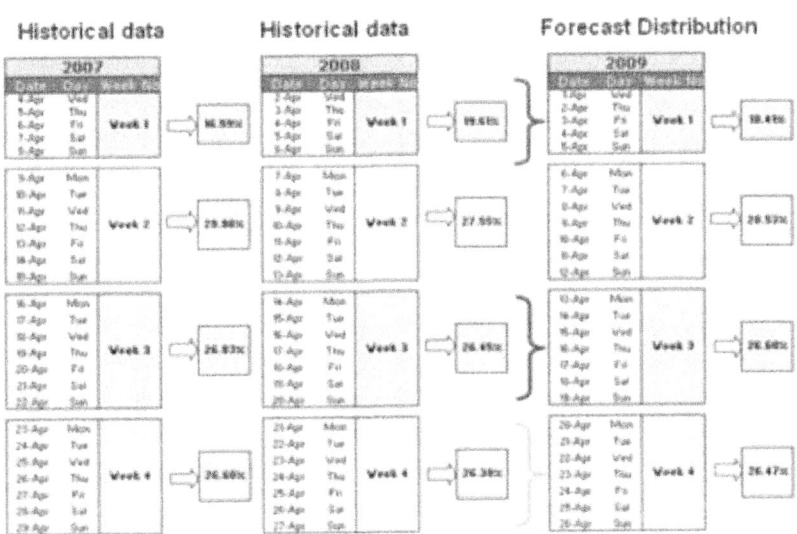

Seasonality Factors

When a repetitive pattern is observed over time, the offered transaction series is said to have seasonal behavior. Seasonal effects are usually associated with calendars, and seasonal variation is frequently tied to yearly cycles. Seasonality of business for different times of the year is shown in the graph below: Increase in transaction volume from April and decrease in transaction volume from September and another small increase in transaction volume in December and January. Similarly, for each business that gets its effects on the season will show such patterns.

Seasonality analysis

Seasonality analysis is calculated by adjusting to time series data due to variations at certain periods, and for this adjustment, we use the seasonal index factor. The following is an example.

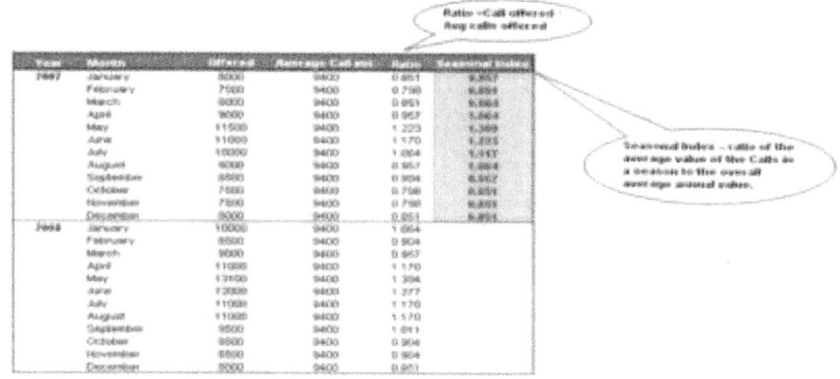

Here, the seasonal index is the ratio of the average value of the item in a season to the overall average annual value.

Example: Average of January 2007 ratio to January 2008 ratio is (0.851 + 1.064)/2 = 0.957

i.e. If Year 3's average monthly Transactions offered is expected to be 50,000 Transactions.

Forecasted Transactions January 2009 = 50,000 X 0.957 = 47,850 Transactions and Forecast Transactions May 2009 = 50,000 X 1.309 = 65,450 Transactions. That's all, simple as that.

Forecasting Techniques

There are two major methods used in this namely: Statistical techniques (Quantitative Techniques) and Judgmental Techniques (Qualitative Techniques)

Statistical Techniques (Quantitative Techniques)

Statistics is the study of the collection, organization, analysis, interpretation, and presentation of data. It deals with all aspects of data including the planning of data collection in terms of the design of surveys and experiments. (Thanks to Wikipedia for the definition). When we use this data and some methods to conclude, then we call it a statistical way of concluding. One of the main techniques used in statistical techniques is time series. Casual Method is also important, which won't be discussed here.

Time Series Methods

Time series methods apply historical data as the basis for estimating future outcomes. There are many methods subsume in this: Moving Average, Weighted Moving Average, Exponential Smoothing, Kalman Filtering, ARMA Method, ARIMA Method, Extrapolation, Trend estimate and so on. Here in this book, I will be explaining about the first four because of their importance.

Moving Average

Moving average (rolling average /.running average) is a calculation that analyses data points by creating a series of averages of different subsets of the full data set. In other words, it's a group of averages. If we are fixing a 3months Moving Average, then every entry is looked as an average of previous 3 months.

Month	Demand	3-month Moving Average
1	650	
2	700	
3	810	
4	800	(650+700+810)/3 = 720
5	900	(700+810+800)/3 = 770
6	700	(810+800+900)/3 = 837
7		(800+900+700)/3 = 800

This method of forecasting is used to smoothen out the spikes. Where there is a high volume, this method can be used to smoothen the curve instead of considering that exception,

Moving Weighted Average,

Moving weighted average method is simple and widely used in forecasting. We saw the application of this method in the interval wise volume allocation. The transaction arrival distribution % at the interval level for Monday is derived after applying moving weighted average for the last 4 week Mondays. Generally, more weightage is provided for the most recent weeks. Most common weighted average logic applied is 40%- 30%- 20% - 10% values from most recent week to fourth previous week.

Exponential Smoothing,

This method is similar to the previous as it is also used to even the numbers. However, unlike Moving Average, exponential smoothing is commonly used for economic and financial market data. Also, this method can be adopted wherever the discrete set of data is used. However, this method should be applied only to the data where there is no seasonal trend or systematic trend.

Best option to understand this is an example.

Month	Demand	Exponential Smoothing
1	650	
2	700	0.1*650+0.9*650 = 650
3	810	0.1*700+0.9*650 = 655
4	800	0.1*810+0.9*655 = 670.5
5	900	0.1*800+0.9*670.5 = 683.5
6	700	0.1*900+0.9*683.5 = 705.2

Here, X0 = 650, X1 = 700, X2 =810, so on.... where 'α' is the smoothing factor (0 < α <

1) Formula for Smoothing is

S0= X0

S1= (α x X1) + (1-α) X0... so on.

Where α is the smoothing factor, and 0 < α < 1

Judgmental Techniques (Qualitative Techniques)

Judgmental Techniques are subjective. Unlike Statistical Techniques, this method does actively involve number but decides on the inputs from the opinions and judgments of customers & experts. This method is applied mainly when there is no historical data (no Statistical Techniques can be applied without data) and for long-term decisions, where accuracy, can be, to an extent, relaxed. Few main techniques used in this are 'Delphi Method', 'Scenario Building', 'Market Survey', and so on. We shall quickly walk through Delphi technique since that will help in our type of forecasting scenarios.

Delphi Method

This method is commonly used in forecasting when there is a lack of appropriate data available to run a Quantitative Analysis. The idea is to collect expert opinions in a structured manner. It recommends at least 5 to 20 experts in the relevant area who are to always backup their submissions with justifications. Furthermore, when the feedback is consolidated, ensure that all the experts' opinion should be given equal weights.

Tips & Tricks in Forecasting

A Great Forecaster should know how to do a forecasting from scratch in a spreadsheet, without using any fancy WFM system

Anyone can forecast, if the means for an accurate background work is on the ground. However, you can't depend on a tool's past accuracy for future events. Accurate forecasting does not immediately confer ingenuity on you even if you deserve to be praised for your resourcefulness.

Ability to perform a complete forecasting process on a blank spreadsheet with tons of raw data with the eventual accuracy is second to one. If you are not armed with such aptitude, I have got a word for you – GO GET IT!

- Understand your Historical/Raw Data

Forecasting is foreknowledge. It is an ability to predict prospects. However, it is not a mechanical venture. Just like your day-to-day activities, although they are the same events, they are not carried out in the same way. This applies to forecasting. If you do not take cognizance of the ever-changing nuances of events, forecasting might be a frustrating art to master.

Therefore, it is necessary to be familiar with the internal workings of your historical data. A spike or drop in your volume pattern must matter to you since they affect eventualities. Ask yourself why that spike is there. What caused it? What about that drop? What are the motions? The remaining works will be easy if you can assimilate the art of knowing the trends from your historical data.

- Maintain your own log book

Wikipedia defines a logbook as a record of important events in the management, operation, and navigation of a ship. It must be filled daily as it is necessary for navigation. You are likely not a sailor, still, maintaining your logbook is paramount to the navigation on the sea of forecasting. From the record of assumptions factored and its impact to anomalies observed in your historical data, business intelligence factored in your previous forecasts, the record of these events is essential as they establish future accuracies and expand your decision-making capacities as regards your customers.

- "Walk a different path" or "Think differently."

There is nothing wrong with being familiar with a pattern derived from your understanding of the trends in your historical data. However, be aware of many subtle distinctions like the nature of product volume, fluctuations, and customer's interest, etc. A good forecaster would know when to draw from the experiences of his past and when to ditch the seemingly most favorable pattern to less familiar routes.

- Intimately understand your Volume Drivers.

A good forecaster should always understand the nature of the volume driver, "5 W&1 H Principle" will help (Who, Why, What,

Where, When, How). Understanding your volume drivers, the proposition of each type is critical to a successful forecast as they all affect you handle time and customer tolerance differently.

- Understand your Audience

A good forecaster with an awful presentation of his ideas and rationale that informs his forecasting decision will not be successful. It is not enough to be able to predict the future. You must be able, among other things, to give a delivery of systematic grounds that informs your decision to convince stakeholders.

'Systematic' does not necessarily mean a complex jam of intricateness. What it means is that your delivery must be suited to appeal to your audience's needs, allay their fears, and stabilize their trust. It is all about delivery and knowing your audience. Knowing your audience will provide the schemata for presentation; the same idea can be presented to two audiences in two different ways. For some, they are looking for the complexities. For others, they are gunning for the simplicity.

- KISS Principle

'Keep It Sophisticatedly Simple' –or other variations include, 'Keep It Short and Simple', 'Keep It Simple Sir' or even 'Keep It Simple, Stupid!' Just like the previous point, do not overburden your presentation with obscurities.

Chapter 2:
Scheduling and Rostering

Preparation and planning unquestionably lead to better outputs. For decades, the focus has been on time & attendance, payroll, and other HR applications, but the importance of "relevant time" that will fetch result went ignored.

According to a recent study on workforce scheduling conducted by the Aberdeen Group, 43% of the executives surveyed indicated that their company has no formal scheduling process in place. The report went on to highlight unawareness of employee's scheduling business value as one of the top reasons for the lagging adoption of this crucial workforce management component.

- 21% - Headcount is too small
- 22% - It doesn't apply to our industry/sector
- 22% - No understanding of scheduling business value
- 30% - No buy-in /urgency among senior management
- 05% - others

Staff Schedule or Roster?

'Staff schedule', 'staff roster', 'rota' or 'off-duty' ... all are same! In Visual Rota, the terms schedule and roster mean the same; it's just that in England, the term schedule is never applied to humans, but only for timetables, and machinery. In England, where the program was developed, a staff schedule is known in three different names; 'staff roster', 'staff rota' or more simply as 'the off-duty'. The term 'rota' began in the Roman times and meant a cycle, as in rotation. The first written evidence of using the English word 'rota' was around 1650. The term roster comes from the Dutch word for the gridiron, hence a grid as a pattern of parallel lines. The word in American usage means a list of names, such as officers or regiments, first used around the mid nineteenth century. The appearance of a 'roster' as

A grid has remained unchanged because it is the most efficient method of displaying staff names, dates and shifts. The term 'shift schedule' will be used in this book.

What is Scheduling?

The aim of employee scheduling is to put the right employees in the right jobs at the right times to meet the business demands. This is a simple process but important as well.

Scheduling encompasses three main functions. They are:

- Determination of Scheduling Preferences
- Incorporation of Scheduling Preferences
- Schedule Distribution and Confirmation

Determination of Scheduling Preferences

In determining the workload and coverage goals, you are predicting the demands for your products or services while you utilize it to know how many employees are needed at different time intervals over the scheduling period. After all, when you are waiting for your turn at the reservation counter in a long queue and the reservation clerk takes a break, how would you feel? Therefore, it is important that you ensure there is a sufficient amount of people scheduled to handle the expected volume/customers.

In each business, employees are bound to perform certain duties that are based on business demands such as confirm hotel reservations for the customer, handle the number of calls received, manufacturer quotas assigned to them, security patrol routes, etc. As a scheduler, you need to understand the need of your business and the duty of each employee. When defining business demand, you need to address some key questions.

What are the drivers for your business demands? By identifying these drivers, you can evaluate and forecast their effect to staffing requirements. For examples, if you are running a call center, your drivers would be the number of calls to be answered, the Average Handle Time (AHT), and the required service level. For hotel housekeeping, it can be the number of rooms to be processed, so on.

Do your business demands vary according to the time of day? Identifying the peaks and valleys and the period over which demands vary helps to understand the cyclical nature of your business needs. Once the demand pattern has been established, you can appropriately schedule shifts that cover the demand. For example, a fast food restaurant will be busier between 11 am to 1 pm or call volumes for emergency services will be lower at nighttime.

Which tasks are required to satisfy your business demands? Tasks are usually defined regarding starting time and duration, or a time window that the task must be completed in, the skills required to perform the task, and locations (if applicable). For scheduling purpose, you can combine individual tasks into task sequences that could be done by one person (e.g. multiple chats transaction at a time- "Concurrency").

You can use your operational knowledge, sales forecasts, confirmed orders, call history, etc. to forecast business demands and create a profile for the scheduling. From this profile, you translate business demands into coverage (head counts, positions, or skills) for each time of the day. Depending on your operation, you might be translating your business demands to coverage goals based on established productivity, service, or economics standards. Alternatively, in some cases, the number of employees is fixed, and your objective is to make full use of the available resources. How to arrive at employees required are covered in following chapters, where we deal with formulas and Erlang functions.

Incorporation of Scheduling Preferences

Now that you have arrived at the number of employees needed for each period, it's time to design a framework for building the actual schedules. This is the step where the number of shifts, length of shifts, and rotation patterns are defined, as well as the scheme of days on/off (all these scheduling inputs is recommended to be kept as a document which can be referred to next week schedule. This will be of much help if you are doing a schedule for multiple business lines or a different set of groups). We call this framework a schedule plan, which serves as a blue print to build your work schedules.

If your operation requires 24 hours and 7 days (24/7) coverage, you are doing shift scheduling. In this case, pay special attention to shift/work fatigue and shift rotation when designing a schedule plan to provide fair and equitable work schedules to all employees. The critical component in a 24/7 schedule plan is the number of teams (teams and crews are used interchangeably herein) needed to cover the work demand. For scheduling purposes, team members are to be assigned to work the same shift and rotation patterns (i.e. team members have the same days on, days off, and rotation schedule). The number of teams dictates the average number of hours worked by each employee. For example, there are 8,736 hours (364 days per year x 24 hours per day) to be worked in continuous 24/7 operations. If you use four teams, then each team member must work an average of 2,184 hours per year (8,736 hours / 4 teams) or 42 hours (2,184 hours / 52 weeks) per week. Plans employing four teams are very popular in 24/7 operations because they closely approximate the 40-hour workweek and provide an optimal balance between work, health and safety, and social demands. The fairest way to schedule employees in a 24/7 environment is to design a schedule in which employees are rotated between shifts.

Most traditional businesses use 8hrs x 5days or 9hrs x 5days schedules in which each person works 8/9-hour shifts for five consecutive days with weekends off. Other variations such as four 10-hour days a week, 12-hour days, three x 13-hour days, split offs (1 or more work days in between offs) or compressed workweek schedules are offered as alternatives. Sufficient gap between two day's work schedules is important, and most people make a mistake in this when rotating the schedules or weekly off.

You must also take into account other constraints when selecting the shift length and the pattern of days on/off. Employment laws and regulations, union, and company rules may restrict the number of consecutive workdays and hours worked or require a minimum rest period between assignments. Pay attention to them so that you will know your boundaries to create an ideal schedule for your business.

While designing a scheduling framework may be time-consuming, a well-designed schedule plan will save you money and boost employees' morale. Once a plan is created, you can keep it as a template and make modifications to it as in required. There is no universal scheduling plan that works for every situation, you create one, and make tweaks until it meets the requirements.

Schedule Distribution and Confirmation

To create work schedules, simply assign your employees to the corresponding shifts in the schedule plan. Do this using information on employee availability, skills, labor rates, and the required number of employees for each period. The goal here is to build the best possible schedule that matches the number of employees scheduled to the ideal number of employees required while satisfying labor rules and employee preferences as much as possible. Seniority, skills required for the different positions being scheduled, planned time-off days, restrictions on the minimum and maximum work hours, and employee preferences are some of the employee's characteristics to be considered when assigning employees. You should set up a hierarchy for these constraints, so you know which one will take precedence when there are conflicting constraints. If you are going for that, shift rotation is applied at this stage; also team wise performance and schedule adherence can give you more insights on which team can come during the peak and valley period of the day for better results.

Break Schedules, Training schedules, and all other off work activities also need to be factored into your schedule to get close to reality schedule. However, ensure that you have sufficient staffing during your peak volumes. On break schedule, don't forget to give at least 1hr difference for the first break from the work start time/end time and sufficient gap between other breaks.

Continual review and refinement of the planned schedule are often needed due to last minute changes in business demand and employee availability. When an employee call in sick or business demands goes high, you need to be able to quickly bring in on-call employees or locate a substitute with the same qualification. Likewise, when the actual business demand falls below what was predicted, you should evaluate the cost impact and reassign the affected employees or send them home if required. If suggestions of whom to be called at what situation can be provided along with the schedule, then you will be moving an extra mile.

Erlang

The Erlang is a dimensionless unit that is used in telephony as a measure of load on service-providing elements such as telephone circuits. (For example, a single cord circuit has the capacity for 60 minutes in one hour. If one hundred six-minute calls are received on a group of such circuits, then the total traffic in that hour is six hundred minutes or 10 Erlangs). This same principle can be used in scheduling, for finding the work force required in each period of the day.

Erlang formula (Erlang B and Erlang C) was developed by A.K. Erlang, after whom the Erlang measure of traffic density and the Erlang programming language were named. Erlang C has become the best traffic modeling formula used in call center scheduling to calculate delays or predict waiting times for callers. Let us quickly see how it will be useful for you to plan your resources correctly.

Erlang B

Erlang-B, also known as the Erlang loss formula, is a formula for the blocking probability that describes the probability of call losses for a group of identical parallel resources (telephone lines, circuits, traffic channels, or equivalent). The formula was derived by Agner Krarup Erlang and is not limited to telephone networks since it describes a probability in a queuing system (albeit a special case with some servers but no queuing space for incoming calls to wait for a free server). Hence, the formula is also used in certain inventory systems with lost sales.

The formula applies under the condition that an unsuccessful call because the line is busy, is not queued or retired, but instead really vanishes forever. It is assumed that call attempts arrive following a Poisson process, so call arrival instants are independent. Further, it is assumed that the message lengths (holding times) are exponentially distributed, although the formula turns out to apply to general holding time distributions.

In simple terms, this method is used to identify the lost opportunity and hence, less used in Scheduling but more in marketing and sales segments.

Erlang C

The Erlang C formula expresses the probability that an arriving customer will need to queue (as opposed to immediately being served). Just as the Erlang B formula, Erlang C assumes an infinite population of sources, which jointly offer traffic of Erlangs to N servers. However, if all the servers are busy when a request arrives from a source, the request is queued. An unlimited number of requests may be held in the queue in this way simultaneously. This formula calculates the probability of queuing offered traffic, assuming that blocked calls stay in the system until they can be handled. This formula is used to determine the number of agents or customer service representatives needed to staff a call center, for a specified desired probability of queuing. However, the Erlang C formula assumes that callers never hang up while in queue that all calls begin and end in the same time period being considered, and that callers never try to call back after having hung up while in the queue. These deficiencies make the formula predict that more agents should be used than are really needed to maintain the desired service level.

-Courtesy goes to wiki for the Definitions

Let us understand how to apply this in the scheduling process. My views about Erlang is that anybody who can type in the syntax of the formula and fill in the necessary segments can get the results, but a basic understanding is required for this.

Erlang calculations are based on few assumptions, if you understand the assumptions, then you will know how to feed your inputs to the formula for the desired output. (e.g., assuming that the Erlang factors 1hr data and you have 30mins data, you need to multiply your data by 2 before feeding it in.) If you are not using any other automated tool for scheduling, you would be using some spreadsheets, and hence, in the forthcoming chapter, I would clarify about Erlang functions used in MS Excel ('ErlangXL97' is the add-on, Google it for your free download). I shall quickly walk through few of the functions needed by schedulers from this.

Abandon Function

Function Abandon (Agents As Single, Abandon Time As Single, CallsPerHour As Single, AHT As Integer) As Single

Agents: This is the number of agents available

Abandon Time is time in seconds before the caller will normally abandon CallsPerHour is the number of calls received in one hour period

AHT (Average handle time) is the call duration including after call work in seconds e.g. 180

This formula returns the percentage of calls that will abandon after the abandon time given. It is assumed that callers will wait for an answer and only abandon if waiting longer than the abandon time.

e.g. =Abandon (8, 30,100,180) returns a value of 0.09 (9%)

Agents function

Function Agents (SLA As Single, Service Time As Integer, CallsPerHour As Single, AHT As Integer) As Integer

SLA is the % of calls to be answered within the Service Time period e.g. 0.85 (85%)

Service time is target answer time in seconds e.g. 15

CallsPerHour is the number of calls received in one-hour period

AHT is the call duration including after call work in seconds e.g. 180 (3 minutes) Returns the number of agents required to achieve the correct SLA. e.g. =Agents (0.85, 15,100,180) returns the value of 8

AgentsASA function

Function AgentsASA (ASA As Single, CallsPerHour As Single, AHT As Integer) As Integer

ASA is the average speed of answer in seconds

Service time is target answer time in seconds e.g. 15

CallsPerHour is the number of calls received in one-hour period

AHT is the call duration including after call work in seconds e.g. 180 (3 minutes) Returns the number of agents required to achieve the correct ASA. e.g. = Agents (15,100,180) returns the value of 8

ASA Function

Function ASA (Agents As Single, CallsPerHour As Single, AHT As Integer) As Single Agents: This is the number of agents available

CallsPerHour is the number of calls received in one-hour period

AHT (Average handle time) is the call duration including after call work in seconds e.g. 180

Returns the Average Speed to Answer for the given number of agents.

e.g. =ASA (8,100,180) returns a value of 10

Call Capacity Function

Public Function Call Capacity (No Agents As Single, SLA As Single, Service Time As Integer, AHT As Integer) As Single

No Agents = the number of agents available

SLA = target percentage of calls to be answered e.g. 0.85 = 85%

Service Time = target answer time in seconds e.g. 15

AHT = (Average handle time) is the call duration including after call work in seconds e.g. 180

The Call Capacity function calculates the maximum number of calls that can be processed by the given number of agents.

e.g. =Call Capacity (8, 0.85, and 15,180) returns a value of 103

Fractional Agents function

Function Fractional Agents (SLA As Single, Service Time As Integer, CallsPerHour As Single, AHT As Integer) As Single

SLA is the % of calls to be answered within the service time period e.g. 0.85 (85%)

Service Time is target answer time in seconds e.g. 15

CallsPerHour is the number of calls received in one hour period

AHT is the call duration including after call work in seconds e.g. 180 (3 minutes)

Returns the number of agents (and fractions of agents) required to achieve the correct SLA.

e.g. =Fractional Agents (0.85, 15,100,180) returns the value of 7.83

The implementation of a fractional agent calculation has no validity within the Erlang model, and agents can only be added in whole numbers. It is included for situations where a more accurate costing model of agents is required (To look deep into minor variations).

Fractional Call Capacity function

Function Fractional Call Capacity (No Agents As Single, SLA As Single, Service Time As Integer, AHT As Integer) As Single

No Agents is the number of fractional agents available as a decimal, e.g. 8.5

SLA is target percentage of calls to be answered e.g. 0.85 = 85%

Service Time is target answer time in seconds e.g. 15

AHT (Average handle time) is the call duration including after call work in seconds, e.g., 180 (3 minutes)

The FractionalCallCapacity function calculates the maximum number of calls that can be processed by the given number of agents. The number of agents, in this case, can be a fractional (decimal) number.

e.g. =FractionalCallCapacity (8.5, 0.85, and 15,180) returns a value of 110

The implementation of a fractional call capacity calculation has no validity within the Erlang model, where agents can only be added in whole numbers. It is included for situations where a more accurate costing model of agents is required.

Queued Function

Function Queued (Agents As Single, CallsPerHour As Single, AHT As Integer) As Single

Agents: This is the number of agents available

CallsPerHour is the number of calls received in one-hour period

AHT (Average handle time) is the call duration including after call work in seconds e.g. 180

Returns the percentage of calls that will have to queue.

e.g. =Queued (8,100,180) returns a value of 0.17 (17%)

Queue Size Function

Function Queue Size (Agents As Single, Calls Per Hour As Single, AHT As Integer) As Single

Agents: This is the number of agents available

Calls Per Hour is the number of calls received in one-hour period

AHT (Average handle time) is the call duration including after call work in seconds e.g. 180

Returns the average queue size.

e.g. =Queue Size (7,100,180) returns a value of 1

Queue Time Function

Function Queue Time (Agents As Single, Calls Per Hour As Single, AHT As Integer) As Single

Agents: This is the number of agents available

CallsPerHour is the number of calls received in one-hour period

AHT (Average handle time) is the call duration including after call work in seconds e.g. 180

Returns the average queue time for those calls that will queue compare with the ASA function that is the average time for all calls including those which get answered immediately.

e.g. =Queue Time (8,100,180) returns a value of 60 (1 minute)

Service Time Function

Public Function Service Time (Agents As Single, SLA As Single, CallsPerHour As Single, AHT As Integer) As Single

Agents = the number of agents available

SLA = target percentage of calls to be answered e.g. 0.85 = 85%

CallsPerHour = the number of calls received in one hour period

AHT = (Average handle time) the call duration including after call work in seconds e.g. 180

The service time function calculates the average waiting time in which a given percentage of the calls will be answered. This can be considered to be the reverse of the SLA function.

e.g. With 8 agents, 100 calls per hour with an average handle time of 180 seconds the time in which 85% of calls will be handled will be: =Service Time(8,0.85,100,180) returns a value of 7 seconds

SLA Function

Function SLA (Agents As Single, Service Time As Single, CallsPerHour As Single, AHT As Integer) As Single

Agents: This is the number of agents available

CallsPerHour is the number of calls received in a one-hour period

AHT (Average handle time) is the call duration including after call work in seconds e.g. 180

Returns the actual service level achieved for the given number of agents e.g. =SLA (8, 15,100,180) returns a value of 0.87 (87%)

Utilization Function

Function Utilization (Agents As Single, CallsPerHour As Single, AHT As Integer) As Single

Agents: This is the number of agents available

CallsPerHour is the number of calls received in one-hour period

AHT (Average handle time) is the call duration including after call work in seconds e.g. 180

Returns the utilization percentage for the given number of agents.

e.g. =Utilization (8,100,180) returns a value of 0.63 (63%)

Tips, Tricks & Facts about Scheduling

Tip#1

It is not necessary to adhere strictly to all the interval requirements but the daily SL requirements are to be given due priority. The fact is that when staffing is based on a fixed staffing level for each interval, then, considerable overcapacity might occur at certain times, because the length of shifts and relatively short peaks in traffic load cannot be matched. Similarly, under capacity occurs in the few short peak intervals if staffing is not matched. Thus the "best" shift mixture not only satisfies the staffing level at all times but around peaks it exceeds this level because we cannot hire agents for the peaks only. A good solution is allowing a low SL for certain intervals, as long as the SL constraint is satisfied on average over the whole day.

Tip#2

More often, a multitude of different possible shifts with varying lengths is preferred to restricted number of shifts with fixed length. Then there are many different good solutions with different mixtures of shift lengths. But shift lengths are often part of the contracts that employees have; the opted combination possibly depends strongly on the preferences and contracts of the employees. Thinking the other way around; the decision on which type of contract to offer to an agent is an important decision with consequences for the scheduling step, as well as to costs. Small shift lengths make scheduling easier, and avoids unnecessary overcapacity. On the other hand, more agents have to be hired in total in the case of short shifts, and therefore overhead costs (such as training and monitoring costs) are higher. Very long shifts reduce the efficiency of agents too.

Tip#3

If your organization provides transportation, then you have a high responsibility to contribute to some cost saving. When two agents use car-pooling to get to work, they should have the same shifts. This fact should be taken into account in the shift determination step: one shift, with the proper requirements, should be chosen at least twice. We see that agent preferences, that usually come into play while making rosters, already play a role in the shift determination step. This calls for an integration of both steps.

Chapter 3:
Real Time Adherence

Monitoring of Real Time Adherence enables organizations to precisely understand what is happening in the business. This is a very crucial part in the management of a workforce. Real Time Adherence allows a business to fine-tune its activity. Once you know what is happening in real time with continuous alerts-on deviations, prevention is possible before a problem occurs. In other words, the more you use Real Time Adherence, the more accurate your forecasts and schedules become.

This segment has enabled traditional work force management to move to more dynamic processes. Real time insights about the execution of plans, the challenges (operational difficulties) faced and changes required in the further plan, etc. will enable the scheduling and forecasting to be more realistic. This reiterates the importance of Real Time adherence management in the WFM segment.

Petals of Real Time Management

Real Time Management is a vast topic dealing with multiple activities associated with it. Any activity handled in real time, which will add value to the business can be considered as real time management but for a structured approach; let's segment it into three parts namely, Monitoring, Control, and Reporting.

Monitoring

Monitoring or looking out for anomalies in Real time is one of the primary duties of an RTA Personnel (the person who is doing Real Time Management can be termed as RTA personnel. There are different names used in different industries such as Duty officer, Manager on Duty (MOD), CCOD (Call Center operations desk), CCO (Call Center Officer), Queue Manager, etc. Few activities of an RTA personal in Real time monitoring are given below.

Queue Management

This is a common term used in ITES business. This segment is utilized maximally in call center industry; therefore, I would strive to elucidate the concepts in the context of Call center industry. Making an employee more productive will be the primary objective of an RTA personnel. Taking an example from a Call center industry; the employees' logs into the telephony system to support the inbound/outbound customers while an RTA personnel ensures that those employees are maximally productive at all times. To achieve this, there will be enabling tools such as AVAYA CMS Supervisor for Avaya Networks, Symposium for Nortel switch, WFM Aspect tool or in some cases, internally developed queue-monitoring tools. These tools will have a refresh delay (2 sec, 10sec, 60 Sec, 2mins, etc.) and in that time, the state of each associate who has logged in will be shown and a real time view of the overall computed values will be provided for a number of parameters like AHT, ACW, Hold times, Service Levels, Abandonment % and Associate Login Times.

Monitoring will be effective only if accompanied by controls i.e. the values in real time are compared against predefined triggers which are laid down in consultation with the business stake holders. If the measured parameter exceeds the laid down trigger, control action is initiated. The triggers with the required control action are maintained in a document called the Trigger Table. This will act as a guideline for Queue monitoring. A Sample Trigger Table is given below.

Parameter	Trigger	Escalation Point	Escalation Method
AHT	>18mins<25Mins	Business Head	Call Email Direct Contact

Queue management is not only limited to triggers on deviations but also empowers you to drive metrics in favor of business needs such as given in next sessions.

Service Level Agreement (SLA) Management

Handle Time management

The RTA personnel ensures that the handling time on the floor is in tandem with the planned Handle Time. This will include a strict vigilance of the Calls handled, ACW and Hold Times. Most of the cases, an RTA personnel ends up having less understanding of how to manage this and raises only triggers on High Handle time scenarios. Raising triggers on high handle time will meet the trigger table requirements, but unfortunately, it will not serve the purpose of control handle time.

Monitoring Off-Call Activity

Also, the RTA personnel manages the off-call activities or activities performed during the scheduled working hours. Off-call activities imply any activity where the employee has to be moved out of the seat thus creating temporary shrinkage or absenteeism. This is managed by RTA personnel since they have more visibility to the volume coming in and how well they can manage it.

Chapter 4:
Seat Capacity Management

There are many other functions which come under work force management depending on the size and structure of the company. Few are seat planning, budget estimate team, reports team, automation team, Robotics Process Automation (RPA) team and so on. In this book, I focus on Seat planning.

Seat Planning

This section of the book contains the outlay of the Seat Management Process or SMP. The primary objective of the SMP is to simplify and streamline the entire process of Seat allocation, Cost calculation per seat and management. Once implemented, Seat Management Process standardizes an efficient and optimized seat allocation process across the organization.

Recommended process in Seat planning

1. **Locking Seat Forecast**

Locking Seats Forecast (LSF) is recommended to cater for the program's need effectively and efficiently. Businesses or departments have to lock their seat requirements 90 days in advance to balance the demand/requirement and availability of seats across the facility and to avoid any contingencies. LSF should be made available to all holding positions above middle-level managers to propose the locking forecast 90 days in advance.

Recommended Mandatory procedures for successful LSF:

Businesses or departments should be able to upload their locking forecast, 90 days in advance, from the 19th to the last day of the month or similar dates as per the financial cycle of the organization.

Example: The seat projections for the month of January 2018 can be uploaded from 19th October 2017 to 31st of October 2017.

Seat Projections are to be raised 90 days in advance by Business or department leads in sync with budget numbers.

Example: Locking seat numbers for January 2018 should be given on or before 31st of October 2017.

Additional seats, over and above the locking forecast may be raised using Seat Incident Form (will be covering in later sections), and the same will be allotted as per availability.

In case the business or department fails to upload locking forecast within the given time frame, locking forecast of the previous month is to be considered. This process will help reduce the unnecessary wastage of effort if there is no change and will make the process lean.

Example: If the locking forecast for January 2017 is not updated, the locking forecast provided for December 2016 by the business or department should be considered for the next month.

Seats considered for Billing should be based on Actual Usage {Weighted Average Method - No. of days, the no. of seats used}

2.   Seat Indent

Whenever a business or department requires a new/additional seat, the head of the concerned department need to submit the form along with all the details (including seat specifications, special constraints & technical details).

The Seat Indent Form should reflect the complete information about the program's seat requirement. The SIF must be filled at least 3 weeks before the requirement date/7days in advance in case of a ramp up of an existing business or department. The following information must be duly captured when submitting the SIF to the Seat Planning Team features:

Mandatory information that needs to be captured in SIF:

- Business/Department name Support hours
- Effective Date & Time
- No. of seats required (Production / Support / Room / Cabins/ Labs) Specification of hardware & software required by each request

o Example: Processor, RAM, Optical Drive, Graphic Card, Break-Me PC, Specific software used by the business/department and any other specific details in accordance with the SOW (statement of work as agreed by client)

Optional information that is recommended to be captured in SIF:

- Facility / Floor / Wing
- Constraints & Special requests
- Additional comments, if any

It is always recommended that in the case of requisition of additional seats (over and above planned), the request must be accompanied by a proportionate revenue increase, which will act as a business justification for the system. After the receipt of the SIF along with the details of the business, it will be analyzed by the Seat planning Team.

If there are any discrepancies between the information regarding the manpower required (production and support) reflected in the budget and the business's request, a clarification would be sought from the Budget team. The head of the department, which requested this, will have to discuss the difference with the budget team.

Once the indent numbers are agreed upon by the budget team and the business, the same numbers have to be intimated to the Seat Planning team. After the verification of the exact figures with regards to (additional) Manpower required/Seats required (production and support), the Seat planning team would allot or arrange the same number of seats to the business or department along with the following details:

- Facility, Floor and Wing wise breakup of the allotted seats along with a detailed Floor Map.
- A copy of the above information will also to be sent to IT department for program specific hardware and software installations.
- If there is a need to bring program specific changes to the infrastructure (e.g. secured area/restricted access), it should be communicated to the Administration team / IT team for necessary action.

Once the indent is agreed upon and the seats are allocated, the turnaround time should be around 2 weeks for the Seat Planning team and the IT team to initiate and provide the program specific hardware and software requirements.

3. **Surrender of Seats**

It is understood that the seat requirement, for any business or department, is dynamic in nature and it varies depending on the volumes and the revenues. In view of this dynamic nature of program's seat requirements, the Seat Planning team has devised the Seat Surrender Process.

If the program's seat requirement goes down, it becomes imperative to surrender the unused seats immediately so that the business's profitability does not suffer any negative impact. To do so, the business head needs to submit the Seat Surrender Form duly filled with the following details:

Mandatory information that needs to be captured in SSF:

- Business/Department name
- Effective Date & Time (Time Zone)
- No. of seats surrendered with breakup (Production/Support/Room/cabin/lab) Facility
- Port Numbers

4. Role of IT

IT team will ensure that the basic Hardware/Software, like System & phones (as per requirement) are installed on all seats allotted by Capacity Planning Team and taken back to stock when the same is surrendered.

5. Billing Input

Billing of seats will be done on the basis of a total number of seats allocated to the department or business. The seats billed for the month is calculated as follows:

Seats Billed = Actual Usage {Weighted Average Method - No. of days, the no. of seats used}

If during any stage, IT/Seat Planning team finds that one of the surrendered seats is being used by the program, these seats will be billed for that month onwards, and the same update would be sent to the Finance department as well. An update regarding the same will also be sent to respective programs.

6. Billing costs

It has been proposed to develop a uniform billing regime across the organization. As per the Uniform Billing Rate, all the production seats (including production and support) will be billed at one rate. This will bring in transparency in the program's revenue generation and profitability.

There are two costs associated with seats. Details of the same are as follows:

1. Connectivity costs: Connectivity cost is different from Voice and Non-Voice based programs.

2. All other overhead costs which are variable in nature and varies on a monthly basis.

The following example illustrates billing for a voice-based program with a total 100 seats, of which 80 seats are production seats and the remaining 20 being used for support:

	No. of Seats	Rate in INR	Total cost in INR
Connectivity Cost	80	A	80 * A
Overhead Cost	100	B	100 * B
		Total	(80*A) + (100*B)

Any seat that may be blocked by or for the business should be billed as actual.

Following example illustrates this clearly:

If a department has 100 seats available on the floor allotted to that department but requires only 96 seats and the department's/client's requirement does not allow any other department to take over those unutilized seats, these seats will be billed for that department. However, the billing will be done only for the overhead costs (not including the connectivity costs).

7. Sharing Costs

If in case the seat is occupied by a single department, the cost of the seat will be billed against that department, immaterial of production or support. However, if need arises, the department will have to share the seats with other departments if the type of work performed accepts this option.

In this case, the cost per seat should be shared proportionately.

Example:

If a seat is occupied for a total of two shifts on a day between two departments, wherein department A occupies the seat for one shift and department B for the other, then the cost will be shared as follows:

Department A- 70 % of the total seat cost occupied in night shift (Primary)

Department B – 30 % of the total seat cost occupied in day shift (Secondary)

8. Billing methods

Around the 3rd working day of every month, the total number of seats occupied by the department should be sent to respective department heads for their reference. However, please be informed that this intimation activity is for reference purposes only and no change request should be considered on this.

The total number of seats occupied by the department should be sent to the Finance department on the 5th working day of every month (or respectively decided by the management) by the Seat Planning team. These figures will, purely, be based on the number of seats allotted as per the SIF, and it will be binding. No change in these figures should be accepted for proper operation.

Expansion & Surrender/Ramp down

Expansion:

-

1. Modification of existing seats

The Seat Planning team should be consulted in all matters pertaining to expansions and modifications. Concerned entities (Management/ Department/Admin/IT etc.) should intimate the Seat Planning team about the exact nature of modifications/expansions and the possible impact that this change may have on the seating capacity of the concerned facility.

Any changes or requirements to the infrastructure will have to be discussed with the Seat planning team. This team, in turn, will interact with the Admin to effect the changes which will sequentially coordinate with the Seat planning team alone for changes that may happen in the infrastructure. No changes will be effected without the mutual consent of the seat planning team and admin team. When requirement emerges, IT division will also coordinate to make necessary changes as demanded by the programs or departments. This is to ensure that the plans and maps are in alignment at all points of time. The following is the proposed model to be followed in such cases:

- Concerned entity informs the Seat Planning Team
- The Seat Planning team initiates a coordinated communication between all the concerned departments.
- After a consensus is reached, Admin initiates the necessary modifications (as instructed by Seat Planning Team) in the structure and informs IT and Seat Planning Teams on completion of the same.
- Seats are allotted to respective department, and the IT sector is instructed to carry out the installation of necessary hardware and software requirements.

- After the completion of the same, IT informs that Seat Planning team and the respective programs.
- Once the seats are ready, the same would be updated in the records or tools (if any).

This model will help to reduce the turnaround time required for these modifications, with the Seat Planning Team acting as the coordinating agency.

2. Adding new facilities

The addition of new facility involves a lot of ground work. Therefore, it is advisable that the Seat Planning team be consulted whenever the need of adding a new facility is felt by the management. The Seat Planning team in addition to the budget team and the business development & the marketing team will provide specific inputs regarding the total seating capacity that may be required in the new facility. These inputs should help the management to decide the total number of seats to be considered for the new facility.

In this case, a modified version of the model proposed earlier can be used for efficient outputs:

- The Seat planning team in conjunction with the Budget team and the Business Development & Marketing team are informed about the decisions to add a new facility.
- These three agencies work in tandem to arrive at a consensus regarding the true capacity of the new facility that may be required in near future.

- The numbers thus arrived at are provided to the management to aid in decision making.

After the acquisition of a new facility, the Seat Planning Team would update the relevant tools/records accordingly, following which, the department will be allotted the deserved number of seats as per their requirements. Soon after the technical agencies (e.g. IT) would be informed to install the necessary technical infrastructure for the respective department.

3. **Surrendering a facility:**

Surrendering a facility involves complex changes in the seating plan and configuration at the organization level, and hence the Seat Planning team should be intimated well in advance regarding any such decision.

This will help them as a medial (or intermediary) agency for coordinating the entire transition out of the facility for all the affected businesses or departments without any adverse impact on production. The following is the proposed model to be adhered to in such cases:

- Seat Planning team is instructed about the decision along with the affected department and other agencies e.g. Admin, IT.
- Seat planning team coordinates the entire process with relevant agencies to ensure a smoother transition.
- Technological issues are discussed with involved agencies and a decision is arrived at.

Chapter 5: Productivity Metrics & Formulas

Importance of metrics

Familiarizing oneself with the key metrics and measurements is imperative for your accomplishment as a pioneer in Work Force Management. In this direction, I have set down the primary measures of success/metrics, Formulas & Benchmarks for each domain.

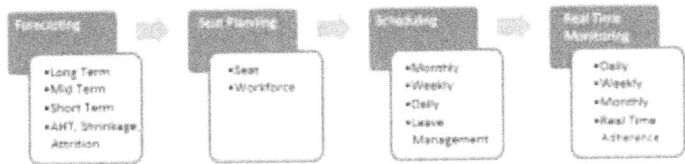

#	Domain	Measure	Definition	Formulae	Benchmark
1	Forecasting	Scheduling Forecasting accuracy (=>90%)	Actual vs. Forecasted transaction volume for the forecast developed schedules for existing staff	100% - ∑(Absolute(Daily Forecast-Daily Offered)) /(Monthly Forecast)	=>90%
2		Staffing Forecasting accuracy (=>90%)	Actual vs. Forecasted transaction volume for the forecast developed to identify required staffing levels to recruit/hire and train staff.	100% - (Absolute(Forecast-Offered)/Forecast)	=>90%
3		Accuracy of Forecasted AHT(+ or - 5%)	Accuracy of the forecasted AHT as measured	100%-(No. of accounts failed on forecasted AHT/No. of accounts forecasted)	+ or - 5%
4		Accuracy of Forecasted Shrinkage (+ or - 5%)	Accuracy of the forecasted shrinkage as measured	100%-(No. of accounts failed on forecasted shrinkage/No. of accounts forecasted)	+ or - 5%
5		Accuracy of Forecasted Attrition (+ or - 5%)	Accuracy of the forecasted attrition as measured	100%-(No. of accounts failed on forecasted attrition/No. of accounts forecasted)	+ or - 5%
6		Coverage % (=100%)	% of accounts covered globally for forecasting (Quarter on Quarter)	Total no. of accounts in scope /Total no. of global accounts	=100%
7		Internal Customer	Satisfaction of the internal customer	No. of parameters	>=90%

#		Metric	Description	Formula	Target
		Experience (=> 90%, 5point Scale)	measured on a scale of 1 to 5	where internal customer rated 4 or 5 / Total no. of parameters	
8		External Customer Experience (=> 85%, 5point Scale)	Satisfaction of the external customer measured on a scale of 1 to 5	No. of parameters where external customer rated 4 or 5 / Total no. of parameters	=>85%
9	Seat-Plan	% of HC Indent triggered/ released HC on-time	Percentage of indents that were triggered on time based on cap-plan trigger with lead time of recruitment and training requirement	Total no. of indents that were triggered on time/Total no. of indents to be triggered	>=98% for headcount indents >=95% for headcount releases
10		% of Seat Indent/released triggered on-time (>=95%)	Percentage of indents that were released on time	Total no. of indents that were released on time/Total no. of indents to be released	>=95%
11		% of Accounts in which Agent Utilization is within tolerance level (-3% ~ +5%)	Percentage of accounts planned in which Agent Utilization is within tolerance level	# of accounts planned within tolerance level / (Total Accounts - Accounts not in scope)	-3% ~ +5% from planned agent utilization
12		Seat utilization	Efficiency measure to know how much are the seats utilised	No. of seats used / No. of seats available	Trend YoY comparison done monthly
13		Seat Turns	Ratio of number of seats vs. headcount	No. of manpower / No. of seats used (will be measured in ratio)	Trend YoY comparison done monthly
14		Cost Overrun due to excess staffing & ratios	Additional cost due to excess staffing and ratios	Additional cost due to excess staffing and ratios	LE Delta
15		Coverage % (=100%)	% of accounts covered globally	Total no. of	=100%

				for planning (Quarter on Quarter)	accounts in scope /Total no. of global accounts (no. of opportunities)	
16			**Internal Customer Experience (=> 90% , 5point Scale)**	Satisfaction of the internal customer measured on a scale of 1 to 5	No. of surveys where internal customer rated 4 or 5 / Total no. of surveys received	>=90% done quarterly
17			**External Customer Experience (=> 85% , 5point Scale)**	Satisfaction of the external customer measured on a scale of 1 to 5	No. of surveys where external customer rated 4 or 5 / Total no. of surveys	=>85%
18		Scheduling	**Accuracy & Availability of Seating & HC information**	Accuracy of the seating & headcount as measured	Quarterly basis audit of data for 15 random programs with 5 random check points each.	>=95%
19			**# of Intervals crossing Over threshold (based on Over/Under analysis)**	Variation between forecasted arrival pattern & staff capacity - Over staffing	Actual vs. required - Over staffed	Greater than +10%, for less than 20% of the intervals Less than or equal to +10% for the remaining intervals
20			**# of Intervals crossing under threshold (based on**	Variation between forecasted arrival pattern & staff	Actual vs. required - Under staffed	Not worse than –5%

#		Metric	Description	Formula	Target
		Over/Under analysis)	capacity - Under staffing		
21		On-Time schedule publication with necessary lead time. (=>98%)	% of schedules published on time within necessary lead time	# of schedules published on time/total # of schedules to be published	>=98%
22		Schedule accuracy (>=90%)	Accuracy of the schedules as measured	100%-(No. of schedules failed /Total # of schedules)	=>90% (How to track?)
23		Complaints regarding schedules	Number of complaints regarding schedules from various customers which includes Business Controllers (BC), Service Delivery (SD) & Human Resource (HR)	Number of complaints regarding schedules from various customers which includes BC, SD & HR	Actual
24		Coverage % (=100%)	% of accounts covered globally for Scheduling (Quarter on Quarter) Planned vs. actual	Actual programs covered/ planned coverage for the program (Quarter on quarter, Only in scope programs to be covered in the quarterly plan)	=100%
25		Internal Customer Experience (=> 90% , 5point Scale)	Satisfaction of the internal customer measured on a scale of 1 to 5	No. of surveys where internal customer rated 4 or 5 / Total no. of surveys.	>=90% done quarterly
26	CCOD	Schedule adherence (>=95%)	Adherence to defined schedule	1 – ((Late Login Deviation + Early Logout Deviation)/Schedule Duration)	>=95%
27		Schedule Duration	Ratio of logged in duration vs.	(Logged in Duration/Scheduled	>=98%

		adherence (>=98%)	scheduled duration	Duration)	
28		**Deviation % of planned Productive Aux usage (+ or - 5%)**	Variation of planned Productive Aux within acceptable limits	Planned Productive AUX Vs Actual Productive AUX	+ or - 5% from target
29		**Deviation % of planned Unproductive Aux usage(+ or - 5%)**	Variation of planned Unproductive Aux within acceptable limits	Planned Unproductive AUX Vs Actual Unproductive AUX	+ or - 5% from target
30		**% of Program meeting Service Level (>=90%)**	Percentage of program meeting service level	# of global programs inscope meeting service level / Total # of inscope programs globally	=>90%
31		**Targeted Agent Utilization tolerance level (-3% ~ +5%)**	An efficiency metric typically calculated by dividing the total amount of time a CSR(customer service representative) spends performing productive work (e.g., talk. hold, wrap, and available) divided by the total number of hours the CSR is either logged onto the system or paid.	(Talk time + Hold time + Wrap time) /Staffed time /No. of agents	-3% ~ +5%
32		**Coverage % (=100%)**	% of accounts covered globally	Total no. of	=100%

#		Metric	Description	Formula	Target
			for Real time queue management	accounts in scope /Total no. of global accounts (no. of opportunities)	
33		Internal Customer Experience (=> 90%, 5point Scale)	Satisfaction of the customer measured on a scale of 1 to 5	No. of surveys where customer rated 4 or 5 / Total no. of surveys received	=>90% done quarterly
34		RTA HC vs. Billable HC Ratio	Ratio of RTA HC vs. Billable HC	Ratio of RTA HC vs. Billable HC	Actual Trend
35	Reports & Dashboards	Reporting performance to clients - On time (=> 95%)	Percentage of reports that were sent to the clients on time	Total no. of reports sent on time/Total no. of reports sent (no. of opportunities)	>=95%
36		Reporting performance to clients - Backlog (<= 2cycles)	For reports not sent on time - It measures "How late is late?"	Average cycles late for those reports that are not sent on time	<=2 cycles
37		Reporting performance to clients - Quality (=> 98%)	Accuracy of the reports that were sent to the client	100% - (Defective reports/Total reports sent)	>=98%

Chapter 6: More Tips and Tricks on proven techniques and Strategies in Workforce management

In this section, we shall briskly gaze at few more tips and tricks that ensure a better workforce management. We shall take into account tips and tricks for each of the workforce management strategies.

Tips & Tricks in Forecasting & Scheduling:

- Make sure your forecast is right: One of the bases of workforce management is ensuring that your prediction for the workload is accurate or at least near to being accurate. It is of foremost importance to be able to interpret historical data accurately and in turn, predict the future. The WFM makes one acquainted of the throughput rates.
- Always Make Sure Rotas are balanced: Another pivotal factor to bear in mind is the rotas. It is of high-priority to make certain the balance of rotas. Discrepancies in rotas daily or weekly have loads of negative effects when it comes to workforce management. In many instances, the imbalance in rotas, habitually caused by multiple rotas, is made obvious by daily difference in SLA (Service level agreement) achievements. If a worker can work only once in three days, it is essential to identify the workforce that will cover for the remaining two days.
- Know your Best agents to cut down the cost: It is necessary to know the agents that are faster, and has quicker delivery times. To do this, you can take a random sample of your agents to know their average handling periods. From the result of your sampling, you can review the working strategies and methods employed by the most effective worker and consider if his/her approach can be imparted to other staff. This will help maintain average workload and efficiency in the team.

- Analyze Your SLA achievements: Yes! SLA achievements are good, in fact, most centers are proud of it. If you legitimately want to manage your workforce, you have to investigate on the reason for the SLA achievement. It might be because you just have the adequate number of staff or you are overstaffed which might be a hindrance. If the latter is the problem, you can deploy the excess staff to other departments.

- Always care for and regard the ways and conditions in which your workers like to work. While some prefer break before a meeting, some others might prefer the break after the meeting. Knowing what your workers prefer always ensure better workforce management.

- WFM is a continuous process. No matter what you know about workforce management, you need to be consistent in your quest for knowledge. Try to get more tips and tricks and implement them.

- As well, you should realize that in WFM project, results are mostly seen at the end of the project. Be careful to be patient enough to wait till the end so that you don't miss the result.
- Try as much as possible to always include WFM outboard capabilities. This helps to schedules that ensure maximum efficiency and reduce overtime as much as possible.

To achieve proper workforce management, you have to look upon the following;

- Plan a flexible shift routine among workers to ensure more efficiency and productivity. This serves clients better.

- Don't try to make everyone happy, most of the times, it doesn't work.

- Ensure that you consider determinants that might serve as barriers to your workers like seat capacity, transportation etc. You should put in place strategies to solve the issue as well.

- One thing that is to be expected is change. Be prepared for change and learn to adapt at that point. Make plans about what you can or cannot do, but be flexible.

- Overstaffing might be desired at some points. It helps increase productivity though labor cost might increase. Being understaffed produces fewer results and efficiency.
- It is vital to create forecasts and schedules of your day in case there is change of plans and you need not have to pay for overtime.

Tips & Tricks in Monitoring and Reporting:

- No matter what you do, never forget the basis. Here, the foundation is workforce management which demands that your agents are never forgotten. Appreciate them for their efforts. This encourages and urges them to do more. Despite your powerful or influential role in the company, do not forget your agents.

- It is always crucial to know the strategy to be implemented at a particular point, which is warranted by ACD routing configuration. It is simply determined by WFM planning procedures and not the other way round.

- Be conscious of Wallboards. Wallboards cannot predict what is to happen, it merely explains what is happening at the moment or an event that has happened. Plan your break according to the WFM system.
- If you still run a sandwich trolley, it would be worthy to change the process or cast out so that better productivity can be assured, especially if it is in the morning! To ensure efficiency, you can order individually for workers at their convenient times in order that work rate is not affected.

- At every point, it is imperative to affirm ownership consistently. The head of a team should know his workers by name and be able to ask how the work of the day went? and what is expected of them on a daily basis.

- Do not take the weekly SLA reports into full belief. Whilst these reports can be informative, they hide lots of deficiencies on the workers' part and hence not entirely reliable. A worker might over perform on one day whereas the same person underperforms the next day, yet the weekly SLA reports declare perfection, which is not absolutely true.

- You need to find a way to measure the performance and competence of individual workers. This will help determine who is more efficient and in turn, more valuable.

- The best way to follow up a project or manage a workforce is by getting timely, constant and accurate updates which also manifests the individual effectiveness of workers. An authoritative person should be entrusted with the right to change services whenever necessary. This can be done during break time or activity re-optimization.
- Lastly, it is essential to optimize all data available. One thing is to present facts to managers; another is that these facts are to be clearly stated and easily understandable. Ensure that you are able to interpret available data, establish the root of relevant problems and also resolve them. Always update your historical data.

Conclusion

Just like many other fields of engagement, the workforce management should be approached with the dexterity that it is demanded of it. Aside from the technicalities, one must not forget the central module of operation is human. This 'humanity centre' as regards the workforce management also includes inputs from other fields and issues like psychology, sociology, biology, gender studies, race, religion etc. Therefore, the preceding tips and information should be expanded and enlarged to cleverly fit into other unforeseen events that may not be exactly industrial. Nevertheless, it is certain that an adequate grasp of the information in this book will supply the entrepreneur with all the tools needed for the task.

Key Terms and Glossary:

WFM has some specialized terms and words that you are likely to come across, many of which you've probably seen in this book thus far.

The following is a handy list of some of the terms that are common in the field. You don't have to commit them to memory, but it can be helpful to know what each of them means.

Important terms to know in the field of Workforce Management:

Abandoned Calls – Calls Answered by the telephone switching system (ACD), but before connecting to the live agent the customer had dropped the call.

Absenteeism – A measure of the percentage of staff that are not present during their scheduled shift duration (font)

Absenteeism cost – Cost incurred due to absenteeism, typically includes the cost of overtime, the cost of increased staffing, the cost of lost productivity, associated cost of absenteeism – such as poor service level, reduced revenue etc.

Accuracy – The quality of transaction, the percentage correct, percentage defective etc.

After Call Work (ACW) – It is a compound of Average Handle Time. ACW is the time taken by the Associate or call taking employee for documentation or closure of the additional activities necessary to complete the previous call.

Auxiliary Time (Aux) – Non-telephone time in an employee's scheduled day. This often includes time spent on training, coaching, breaks, meetings, etc. Aux state will be tracked with different codes depending on the ACD system used.

ASA – Average Speed of Answer. The average time taken by the employee to answer the call from the time it is ringing on his/her desk phone system.

Average Talk Time – Yet another component of Average handle time. The time spent by the call taking associate or employee talking with the customer.

Forecasting Accuracy- Forecasting accuracy is defined and must be measured at two levels:

> **Staffing Forecast Accuracy** (e.g. actual vs. forecasted transaction volume for the forecast developed to identify required staffing levels to recruit/hire and train staff)

Scheduling Forecast Accuracy (e.g. actual vs. forecasted transaction volume for the forecast developed schedules for existing staff)

Full-Time Equivalent (FTE) – Usually defined by the entity. It requires standardizing full-time and part-time employees to a full-time equivalent. For example, two part time employees each working half time would be considered one FTE.

Net Promoter Score – The difference between the percentage of customers who are promoters and the percentage of customers who are detractors.

Performance Metrics – Measures used by the associate to track performance, mainly for progress review or coaching or training.

Schedule Adherence – There are multiple definitions of schedule adherence. The numerator and denominator will vary, depending on the definition. Roughly it is the difference between the planned schedule and actual presence.

Scheduling – Assigning associate by period to meet the estimated loaded demand.

Scope of work (SOW) – A definition of requirements created by a client and a call center company that clearly delineates the work product to be delivered by the call center company.

Service level – A measure expressing the percentage of transactions that are responded to in a specified time frame as agreed by SLA.

Service Level Agreements (SLA) – Written contracts or agreement with suppliers or products or service. These usually consist of performance levels and targets mutually agreed upon.

Printed in Great Britain
by Amazon